Animal Classifications

Mammals

Angela Royston

heinemann
raintree

To contact Capstone Global Library, please call
800-747-4992, or visit our web site www.capstonepub.com

Edited by Helen Cox Cannons, Clare Lewis, and
    Abby Colich
Designed by Steve Mead
Picture research by Tracy Cummins
Production by Victoria Fitzgerald
Originated by Capstone Global Library Ltd
Printed and bound in China by Leo Paper Group

18 17 16 15 14
10 9 8 7 6 5 4 3 2 1

Library of Congress Cataloging-in-Publication Data
Royston, Angela, 1945- author.
  Mammals / Angela Royston.
    pages cm.—(Animal classification)
  Summary: "This fascinating series takes a very simple
look at animal classifications, with each book focusing
on a different group of animal. This book is about
mammals: what they do, how they behave, and how these
characteristics are different from other groups of animals.
Beautifully illustrated with colorful photographs, the book
shows many examples of different types of mammals in
their natural environment."—Provided by publisher.
  Includes bibliographical references and index.
  ISBN 978-1-4846-0753-4 (hb)—ISBN 978-1-4846-0760-2
(pb)—ISBN 978-1-4846-0797-8 (ebook) 1. Mammals—
Juvenile literature. 2. Animals—Classification—Juvenile
literature. I. Title.

QL706.2.R69 2015
599—dc23   2014013463

**This book has been officially leveled by using the F&P
Text Level Gradient™ Leveling System.**

Acknowledgments
We would like to thank the following for permission to
reproduce photographs: Capstone Press: Karon Dubke, 27;
Getty Images: Dr Clive Bromhall, 25, Mark Carwardine,
13, 29 Top; Shutterstock: Anan Kaewkhammul, Design
Element, Bailey0ne, 4, CanuckStock, 19, Christopher Elwell,
23, Four Oaks, 15, glenda, 18, Ivan Kuzmin, 7, Jarry, 20, 29
Bottom, Ken Wolter, 12, Kirsanov Valeriy Vladimirovich,
21, lightpoet, 11, Cover, Monkey Business Images, 26, Oleg
Znamenskiy, 6, Seleznev Oleg, 8, 29 Middle, Stuart G Porter,
10, T.W. van Urk, 5, worldswildlifewonders, 17; SuperStock:
Minden Pictures, 14; Thinkstock: Alan Jeffery, 24, Andre
Anita, 9, Jiri Haureljuk, 16, 28, Photoservice, 22.

We would like to thank Michael Bright for his invaluable
help in the preparation of this book.

Contents

Meet the Mammals...4

Body Shape 6

Hair and Fur..8

Cats 10

Sea Mammals.. 12

Giving Birth 14

Marsupials.. 16

Caring for Young... 18

Rodents.. 20

Herds and Packs 22

Monkeys and Apes 24

One Amazing Mammal!...................................... 26

Quiz... 28

Glossary 30

Find Out More... 31

Index.. 32

Some words are shown in bold, **like this.** You can find out what they mean by looking in the glossary.

Meet the Mammals

Dogs, squirrels, sheep, and elephants are all mammals. Mammals are animals that have hair on their bodies and that feed their babies with milk from the mother.

Dogs and humans have lots of hair, so they are **classified** as mammals.

4

Two lambs feed on milk, which they suck from the mother sheep.

Scientists sort living things into groups. This is called **classification**. Each group of living things is different from other groups in particular ways.

Body Shape

Mammals are part of a bigger group called **vertebrates**. This group also includes **reptiles** and birds. All vertebrates have a backbone and a hard skeleton inside their bodies. The skeleton gives their body its shape.

Giraffes have the longest legs and neck of any mammal.

bones in wings

legs

Bats are the only mammals that have wings.

Most mammals have four legs, or two legs and two arms. Bats are mammals, but they have two legs and two wings. The wings are made of long, thin finger bones, with skin stretched between them.

Hair and Fur

A mammal has hair that grows from its skin. Hair protects the skin and helps to keep the mammal warm. Some mammals, such as wolves, have thick hair. Others, such as elephants, have only a few hairs.

A camel's hair protects its skin from the hot sun.

A polar bear lives in the icy Arctic. Its thick hair helps to keep it warm.

Mammals are **warm-blooded**, which means that they make heat using the energy from food. Blood carries the heat all around their bodies.

Cats

Mammals are **classified** into smaller groups and families. The cat family includes big cats, such as lions, cheetahs, and tigers, as well as smaller pet cats. All cats look similar. For example, they have long backs and most have long tails.

A cheetah bends its long back as it runs.

It is easy to see that a lynx is a type of cat.

Cats have sharp claws and sharp teeth. They need them because they are **carnivores**. Carnivores eat meat from other animals.

Sea Mammals

Sea mammals, including seals, dolphins, and whales, live in the sea. Seals have thick fur, but most sea mammals, such as walruses and whales, have almost no hair.

Seals spend some time on land, but they hunt for food in the sea.

The blue whale is the largest animal that has ever lived.

Instead of legs and arms, sea mammals have **flippers,** which they use to swim. Unlike fish, sea mammals cannot breathe in water. They have to come to the surface to breathe.

Giving Birth

Instead of laying eggs, almost all mammals give birth to babies. The babies are small, but have the same body shape as their parents. Some mammals have several babies at a time. Others have one or two.

This dog has six puppies, which all look like her.

An elephant usually has one baby calf at a time.

All mammal mothers make milk in special parts of their body called **mammary glands.** Babies feed on their mother's milk until they are old enough to eat other food.

Marsupials

Kangaroos and koalas are both **marsupials**. Female marsupials have a special **pouch**. A baby marsupial is born when it is still tiny and not fully formed. It crawls into its mother's pouch, where it feeds on milk and grows bigger.

A kangaroo baby is safe in its mother's pouch.

Young koalas stay close to their mothers even after they have left the pouch.

A baby marsupial is called a joey. When the joey is big enough, it leaves the pouch and explores the world.

17

Caring for Young

Mammals take care of their young until they are old enough to look after themselves. Baby mammals stay close to their mothers, who try to keep them safe from **predators**.

Newborn deer can stand and walk when they are only a few hours old.

A tiger cub practices stalking. It moves forward slowly, then pounces.

Baby mammals learn many skills from their mothers. For example, tiger cubs learn how to hunt for food.

Rodents

Mice, hamsters, squirrels, and prairie dogs all belong to a group of mammals called **rodents**. Many female rodents have lots of babies at the same time. A group of babies is called a **litter**.

All rodents have four large front teeth and gnaw their food.

A house mouse can have many litters of babies every year.

Baby rodents grow up fast! A house mouse starts to have her own babies when she is just two months old. She may produce 150 babies a year!

Herds and Packs

Mammals that feed on plants, such as zebra and buffalo, live in large groups called **herds.** Living in a group makes it easier for these animals to stay safe from **predators.** Some mammal predators hunt together in groups called packs.

These zebras watch out for danger as they graze on the grass.

Prairie dogs leave their underground homes to feed.

Smaller mammals, such as **rodents** and rabbits, **burrow** under the ground. For example, prairie dogs live together in huge underground "towns."

Monkeys and Apes

Monkeys, lemurs, and apes belong to a group of mammals called **primates**. Monkeys mostly live high among the trees. They leap from branch to branch and tree to tree.

Some monkeys use their tail like an extra arm or leg to grip onto a branch.

A chimpanzee uses a rock as a tool to crack open nuts.

Apes include humans, so other apes are more like us than other animals. Apes have no tail and can stand on their two back legs.

One Amazing Mammal!

Humans are perhaps the most amazing mammal. Humans can speak, read, and write. They can compose music and invent complicated machines. They can discuss ideas and plan for the future.

Human children take many years to grow up because they have so much to learn!

Humans love and care for other animals. This girl cares for her pet cat.

Humans understand the world better than any other animal. Can we use that understanding to make the world a better place for all animals to live in?

Quiz

Look at the pictures below and read the clues. Can you remember the names of these mammals? Look back in the book if you need help.

1. I am safe inside my mother's **pouch.** What am I?

Answers
1. joey
2. whale
3. camel
4. squirrel

2. I live in the sea, but I breathe in air. What am I?

3. I live in the desert. My hair protects me from the sun. What am I?

4. I am a **rodent**. I have four large front teeth. What am I?

Glossary

burrow animal's underground home; digging an underground home

carnivore animal that eats other animals for food

classification system that scientists use to divide living things into separate groups

classified put into a group according to special things shared by that group

flipper hard, flat part of a sea mammal's body, which it uses to swim

herd large group of animals

litter number of babies born at the same time

mammary gland part of a female mammal's body that can make milk

marsupial mammal that gives birth to young that are not fully formed and continue to grow in the mother's pouch

pouch pocketlike body part on the outside of the body

predator animal that kills other animals for food

primate member of a group of mammals that have hands and handlike feet. Monkeys, apes, and humans are primates.

reptile member of a group of animals that have dry, scaly skin

rodent member of a group of mammals that have four large front teeth, which they use to gnaw food

vertebrate animal that has a backbone and skeleton inside its body

warm-blooded able to make body heat from food

Find Out More

Books

Berger, Melvin and Gilda. *Mammals* (True or False). New York:
Scholastic, 2011.

Schuetz, Kari. *Mammals* (Blastoff!: Animal Classes). Minneapolis:
Bellwether Media, 2013.

Thomas, Isabel. *Marvelous Mammals* (Extreme Animals). Chicago:
Raintree, 2013.

Veitch, Catherine. *Mammal Babies* (Animal Babies). Chicago:
Heinemann Library, 2013.

Web sites

FactHound offers a safe, fun way to find internet sites
related to this book. All of the sites on FactHound have
been researched by our staff.

Here's all you do:
Visit www.facthound.com
Type in this code: 9781484607534

Index

apes 24, 25

baby mammals 4, 5,
    14–19, 20–21
bats 7
birds 6
body shape 6–7, 14

camels 8
carnivores 11
cats 10–11, 27
cheetahs 10
chimpanzees 25
classification 4, 5, 10

deer 18
dogs 4, 14

elephants 4, 8, 15

families 10

giraffes 6
giving birth 14–15

hair and fur 4, 8–9, 12
herds and packs 22–23
humans 4, 25, 26–27
hunting 19, 22

kangaroos 16–17
koalas 16, 17

lynxes 11

mammary glands 15
marsupials 16–17
mice 20, 21
milk 4, 5, 15, 16
monkeys 24

polar bears 9
prairie dogs 20, 23
predators 18, 22
primates 24–25

reptiles 6
rodents 20–21, 23

sea mammals 12–13
seals 12
sheep 4, 5
skeletons 6
squirrels 4, 20

tigers 10, 19

vertebrates 6

walruses 12
warm-blooded 9
whales 12, 13
wings 7
wolves 8

zebras 22